Rules
of the Road

By John Winthrop

ISBN 978-0-9970242-0-3

J Winthrop, Charleston, South Carolina

www.winthropfamily.org

DEDICATION

To grandsons Brad and Robbie -

With the hope that they will develop their own
Rules of the Road as they grow older

AUTHOR'S NOTE

These observations, entitled *Rules of the Road*, are included in a collection of letters to my grandchildren. By way of an introduction only one of these letters is included in this literary effort.

Dear Grandchildren,

Now that I have written a number of letters to you on a variety of topics, let me try an experiment. I will select several topics where you are in the process of developing your own ideas.

I have prepared a list of "bullet points" for each topic. These are my pointers, my ideas, my road map - a road map I do not necessarily follow always - but rather a series of ideas that make sense to me.

Pages have been provided for you to create your own road map for life. You may wish to add other topics, to reduce the list, or to change it in any way you wish.

My hope, of course, is that this exercise will make you think about some important subjects and develop you own ideas about your life and how to live it.

With love,

Grandad

FOREWARD

John Winthrop has taken the time to compile a wonderful collection of personal reflections. He notes that he was only trying to clarify his own thinking when he wrote *Rules of the Road*, but this is a charming and straightforward book full of humor and wisdom.

Senator John Kerry

ACKNOWLEDGEMENTS

Several people have contributed in no small part to this literary effort - among them: Jon-Jon Eraula, original illustrator, currently serving in the U. S. Navy; Mary Howell, tireless assistant, providing administrative support; Shanna McGarry, giving encouragement and creative design to the author's photographs. To all of the above I feel a debt of gratitude.

TABLE OF CONTENTS

Rules
on Children

RULES ON CHILDREN . . .

1) Don't try to create them in your own image; they're different from you and from one another.

2) Try to guide by example, not by force.

3) Give your child an allowance early in life.

4) Have fun together when possible.

5) Spend time together. Children are more important than most of the things you do.

6) Teach children to live within their means. Try to give them as much as you feel you can afford early in their lives so that they can have financial self-respect when they come of age.

7) Teach children to write thank-you notes and sympathy notes while getting them to understand the needs of others.

8) Try to give the occasional present for no particular reason.

9) Let children win in games if their self-image can be enhanced.

10) Hug.

MAKE YOUR OWN RULES:

_____

_____

_____

_____

_____

_____

_____

_____

Rules
on Marriage

RULES ON MARRIAGE . . .

1) Take great care to develop acceptable rules for you both and remember you don't always have to be right.

2) Take time in the selection of a mate. No decision will be more important. Resolve to be best friends . . . to spend time together.

3) Learn to resolve conflicts. Don't hold a grudge.

4) Don't put too much emphasis on romance.

5) Don't put too much emphasis on money.

6) Don't put too much emphasis on power.

7) Put great value on fairness and friendship.

8) Back each other up – with outsiders, with children, with everyone.

9) Pay attention to the spiritual side of your life together.

10) Be gentle.

MAKE YOUR OWN RULES:

_____

_____

_____

_____

_____

_____

_____

_____

Rules
on Learning

RULES ON LEARNING . . .

1) Recognize the importance of intellectual curiosity. This appetite can become insatiable and the rewards can enrich life's journey.

2) Select courses by the great teachers, whatever the subject matter.

3) Don't place too much importance on grades.

4) Be irreverent about the opinions of others. Learn the ultimate truths on your own. Skepticism can be useful.

5) Reach for the interlocking and overlapping stories in music, history, art, the languages, etc.

6) Remember the importance of the computer.

7) Learn to write. Communication with the written word will always be important.

8) Discuss what you have learned with others.

9) Don't be intellectually arrogant.

10) Listen.

MAKE YOUR OWN RULES:

_____

_____

_____

_____

_____

_____

_____

_____

Rules
on Spirituality

RULES ON SPIRITUALITY . . .

1) Look for the relationship between the great religions of the world. They all have much in common.

2) Be tolerant. Don't assume that you have the only pipeline to God. He loves us all.

3) Go to your place of worship spontaneously.

4) Avoid being falsely pious or assuming a higher moral platform than others.

5) Be with your child at bedtime and talk to God together.

6) Try to live in a way that observes the profound need to be kind to one another.

7) Get to know people at your place of worship.

8) Avoid extremism in any religion.

9) Take God very seriously – listen to Him.

10) Pray.

MAKE YOUR OWN RULES:

_____

_____

_____

_____

_____

_____

_____

_____

Rules
on Family

RULES ON FAMILY . . .

1) We merely stand on the shoulders of those who have gone before us. Our ancestors have made our lives easier.

2) Don't dwell too much on past. It can bore others easily.

3) Provide your family with a family tree. Roots from the past and wings for the future can provide inspiration.

4) Remember: you can pick your friends and you can pick your nose, but you cannot pick your family.

5) Let family members know that you love them unconditionally . . . even if it is hard to do so at times.

6) Be a good listener. Try to understand the criticism of other family members. They are not afraid to tell the truth.

7) Understand that sibling rivalries and perceived injustices suffered in childhood tend to last a long, long time.

8) Understand that your mother and father are imperfect, but they do the best they can.

9) Call your mother.

10) Communicate.

MAKE YOUR OWN RULES:

_____

_____

_____

_____

_____

_____

_____

_____

_____

Rules
on Joy

RULES ON JOY . . .

1) Do one thing that's fun every day.

2) Play catch with a child.

3) Listen to the sounds of nature.

4) Go to a baseball game.

5) Pause to smell freshly cut grass in the springtime.

6) Treat yourself to music you love.

7) Wave at children.

8) Share intellect, embrace others, and rejoice without guilt.

9) Don't be afraid to get dirty sometimes.

10) Smile.

<u>MAKE YOUR OWN RULES:</u>

_____

_____

_____

_____

_____

_____

_____

_____

Rules
on Self-discipline

RULES ON SELF-DISCIPLINE . . .

1)   Save a little money each month; live within your means.

2)   Stick to plans, chores, projects and diets.

3)   Reward yourself for achievements.

4)   Consume free time, friendships, and ice cream in moderation.

5)   Don't gossip. Don't litter. Don't push. Don't honk. Don't interrupt.

6)   Be available for others, even if it's inconvenient.

7)   Pay your fair share. Always.

8)   Avoid snooping in the private lives of others.

9)   Don't ever lie.

10)   Share.

MAKE YOUR OWN RULES:

_____

_____

_____

_____

_____

_____

_____

_____

Rules
on Business

RULES ON BUSINESS . . .

1) Keep it simple and do what you do well.

2) Respect the environment in your business ventures.

3) With any investments, pay careful attention to the bookkeeping and to the key people within the enterprise.

4) Strive for excellence through good management, cooperation, and respect for others on all corporate levels.

5) Remember that you are your own best asset.

6) Feel good about being a capitalist.

7) Retain a social conscience. Devote a portion of your earnings to charity. There are plenty of good causes.

8) Find joy in your work. If you are unhappy, change careers.

9) Always try to remain upbeat and enthusiastic.

10) Be tough; be kind.

<u>MAKE YOUR OWN RULES:</u>

_____

_____

_____

_____

_____

_____

_____

_____

Rules
on Money

RULES ON MONEY . . .

1) Enjoy money and provide for your family.
   You can't take money with you.

2) Remember how destructive envy is.

3) Use money as a force for good when possible. Giving money in a creative manner is more challenging than investing wisely.

4) As soon as you are able to enjoy the fruits of your labors, spend money and enjoy the rewards.

5) Have no guilt in earning money.

6) Define and understand your financial objective in life.

7) Fancy cars and fine clothes don't represent good character and kindness of heart.

8) Do not hold money over the heads of others.

9) Give money to your child because you love that child. Do not use it as an incentive for others.

10) Over tip.

MAKE YOUR OWN RULES:

_____

_____

_____

_____

_____

_____

_____

_____

Rules
on Investing

RULES ON INVESTING ...

1) Save as much as you can.

2) Ignore those who boast about beating the market.
   (Nearly no one does every year.)

3) Ignore the quarter-by-quarter performance.
   Focus on the longer term (three to five years).

4) Remember asset allocation (cash, bonds, stocks, real estate,
   fine arts) is more important than stock picking.

5) Keep turnover low; avoid trading (remembering commissions
   do not help performance).

6) Concentrate on selection, not timing.
   (No one can time the market consistently.)

7) Diversify (but don't over diversify).

8) Emphasize quality. (Superior management, strong balance
   sheets and market dominance are valuable criteria in the
   selection process.)

9) Emphasize those sectors providing essential products (finance-
   related, health-related, technology-related, energy-related).
   Keep bonds investment grade.

10) Remember always that money is not the most important thing in life.

MAKE YOUR OWN RULES:

_____

_____

_____

_____

_____

_____

_____

_____

Rules
on the Environment

RULES ON THE ENVIRONMENT …

1) The sun, the moon and the earth are all beautiful –
but we can destroy only this planet.

2) Overpopulation is the root of all environmental degradation.

3) Clean water will become increasingly scarce; cherish it.

4) Fossil fuels are destructive; push mightily for alternative
sources of energy.

5) Wild birds and wild animals enrich our lives; protect both.

6) Americans are champion consumers; we must find a way
to cut back our wasteful habits.

7) Most Americans have too much stuff; we must find a way
to be more generous.

8) Support worthy environmental organizations – with work,
with wisdom, and with wealth.

9) Remember we do not own our land. We must be stewards
for future generations.

10) Plant a tree.

MAKE YOUR OWN RULES:

_____

_____

_____

_____

_____

_____

_____

_____

Rules
on Relationships

RULES ON RELATIONSHIPS ...

1) All relationships are complicated – between countries, between individuals, between husband and wife.

2) Invest more in diplomacy and less in arms, and communicate that message to your representatives.

3) Understand that relationships change – nearly always.

4) Be patient and hope that common sense will prevail in any dispute.

5) Be practical and weigh the cost and benefits of war, of divorce, of cutting someone off.

6) Be loving, if possible. (Make love – not war!)

7) Be kind – remembering the importance of acknowledging the existence of others.

8) Attack a problem together to find a solution rather than attacking each other.

9) Avoid anger; avoid jealously; avoid self-righteousness.

10) Avoid joint ownership.

MAKE YOUR OWN RULES:

_____

_____

_____

_____

_____

_____

_____

_____

www.ingramcontent.com/pod-product-compliance
Lightning Source LLC
Chambersburg PA
CBHW070831100426
42813CB00003B/571